MASTER CLASS

by
**Bruce
Buckingham**

Speed • Pitch • Balance • Loop

To access audio visit:
www.halleonard.com/mylibrary

Enter Code
4434-7008-4386-8034

This book is dedicated to my daughter Emily.

ISBN 978-0-634-00603-6

7777 W. BLUEMOUND RD. P.O. BOX 13819 MILWAUKEE, WI 53213

Visit Hal Leonard Online at
www.halleonard.com

Table of Contents

About the Author

Bruce Buckingham has been a professional musician and music teacher for over 25 years. He joined the staff at G.I.T. in 1980 and has since taught guitar to thousands of students from around the world. Bruce plays guitar in many styles, but specializes in jazz, Latin, blues, and funk. He has played and/or recorded with a number of diverse and notable musicians, including Helen Reddy, John Patitucci, and Michael Jackson. Bruce currently divides his time between live gigs, studio work, and teaching at Musicians Institute in Hollywood, California. He is also working on his own recording project and continues to develop additional instructional products for MI Press.

Bruce can be reached by email at funkybucks@earthlink.net.

Bruce Buckingham

Part One

Brazilian Rhythms

Brazilian music has a certain "swing" that can be only learned through repeated listening and playing. In part one of this book, we'll focus on the rhythms of Brazil and get you playing them right away. In particular, we'll look at several different Brazilian styles, from the relatively simple to the more complex:

Bossa nova, the first style we'll cover, started in Brazil in the late 1950s as an outgrowth of the more traditional samba. In the '60s, it made its way to the U.S. where it caught on big among musicians and listeners alike. (Its influence is still felt today in jazz and pop music around the world.) Guitarist Joao Gilberto and composer Antonio Carlos Jobim were two pioneers of this style, which is in a moderate 4/4 feel. Typically, in a bossa nova guitar part, the thumb plays bass notes on beats 1 and 3 while the fingers syncopate chords against that beat. We'll build up this "chord-and-bass note" technique first with one-bar patterns, then with two-bar patterns and their variations.

Samba is probably the best known of all Brazilian grooves; it started in the early 1900s and continues to this day. Samba is a faster style, typically felt in "2" instead of "4," which gives it a different quality. Nevertheless, many of the patterns learned for bossa nova can also be used for samba, with some modifications. Because it's faster, samba makes extensive use of the thumb-and-fingers "block chord" approach to accompaniment, which lends itself to a unique "constant eighth-note" style.

Partido alto, baião, and *3/4 bossa nova* are three popular variations of standard Brazilian rhythms. Partido alto with its funky accents, the baião with its unique root-5th-root bass pattern, and 3/4 bossa with its elegant connotations, will all serve to round out our understanding of Brazilian "swing."

PRACTICE TIPS

This section contains a lot of patterns; the coordination developed in learning them will be used throughout the entire book.

- All patterns can and should be memorized as soon as they are understood. From then on, "hear" the chords in a rhythmic context and develop the one- and two-bar phrasing with a variety of voicings and harmonic rhythms.

- Practice all examples along with the tracks, in the keys in which they are written. Then, practice the same progressions in other keys by yourself. Practice in as many keys as possible in order to get the feel of each rhythm as well as each progression. (You can tranpose most of the chord voicings just by moving them up or down the neck.)

- These patterns can work in a variety of situations and need to be practiced enough to handle different tempos. You can eventually hear where to improvise if you know the patterns well enough!

- A certain endurance is needed to sustain the constant rhythm at first, but it should begin to flow with practice. Relax and *hear* the patterns.

Chapter 1 BOSSA NOVA

THE ONE-BAR PATTERN

The basic *bossa nova* comping pattern is a one-bar figure that alternates between a bass note played by the thumb and a chord played by the fingers. Coordination between the thumb and fingers is essential to getting the feel of this pattern down—as well as to being able to move on to the other bossa nova patterns.

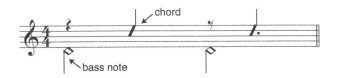

Your first goal should be to become comfortable with this rhythm. Practice the pattern a lot, until you can play any set of chord changes with it. Use any chord voicing you like; the important thing is to keep a steady rhythm feel and to supply the "bass note and chord" type of accompaniment. If you change bass notes, it is usually the root and 5th of the chord that alternate. If you do not have an available 5th in your voicing at the moment, then don't worry about it; just use the root twice.

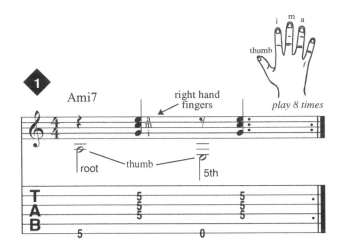

Here are some progressions for practicing the pattern with an alternating bass. These are each "two measures per chord," which allows you to concentrate on the rhythm. These should also give you some ideas for appropriate chord voicings in this style.

These next examples are a bit more challenging: same pattern, but now the chords are changing faster. Again, you can play just the root in the bass, or alternate between the root and 5th in this style.

Now we're cranking! In these next progressions, you have only half a measure, or one bass note, to establish the chord change, so you'll want to stick with just the root in the bass. Notice how active the bass line becomes.

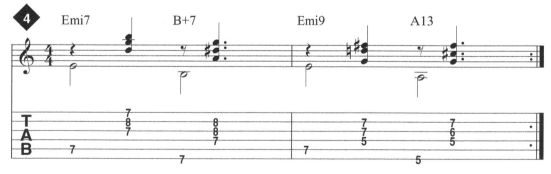

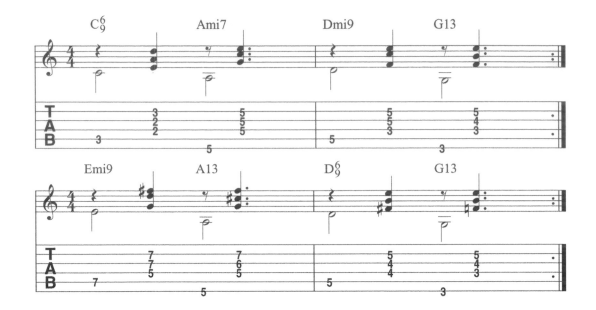

One-Bar Variation

The variation here is the addition of a chord attack on the upbeat of beat 4. This becomes important later as we'll use it for rhythmic and harmonic anticipation—for now, however, just play the same chord through the whole measure.

Harmonic Rhythm

Now that you have the right-hand coordination down and can make your bass notes follow the root (or root/5th) of each chord, you must get used to chord changes that last for various durations—eight beats (two measures), four beats (one measure), or even two beats (1/2 measure). How many beats each chord receives is called the *harmonic rhythm*. Faster harmonic rhythm means that the chords are changing more quickly; slower harmonic rhythm means that you remain longer on each chord.

Use these exercises to get used to changing chords at different harmonic rhythms. Keep your tempo steady and play all voicings cleanly! Use both the one-bar pattern and its variation.

* [2] and [3] are not included on Track 7.

Anticipation

If you're comfortable switching between chords—and your bass notes sound nice and steady—then you're ready for the next rhythmic development. This is called *anticipation*. Anticipation is a concept that runs throughout music, regardless of style, and applies to both rhythm and harmony. Within this Brazilian context, we are speaking mainly about a chord being anticipated on the upbeat, or the "and," of beat 4. This next example is a pattern that "anticipates" the downbeat of the next bar:

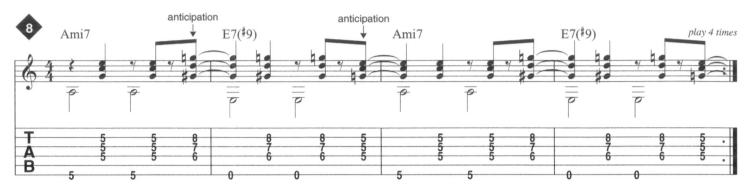

Notice that the E7(♯9) in the second measure is anticipated by actually occurring on the "and" of beat 4 in the first measure. This causes the chord to change slightly ahead of the bass note. This happens again with the Ami7 chord, which is also anticipated on the "and" of beat 4 in measure 2, leading into measure 3 and the bass note. This can continue for as long as you want it to. You may combine this with either of the two one-bar patterns learned so far.

Practice the following chord pairs using this technique. Remember: Chords can be written in slash notation like this, but played with the anticipated feel as it looks above. You must hear the chord first on the upbeat of 4, then the bass note follows on beat 1 of the next measure. Both chords may be anticipated.

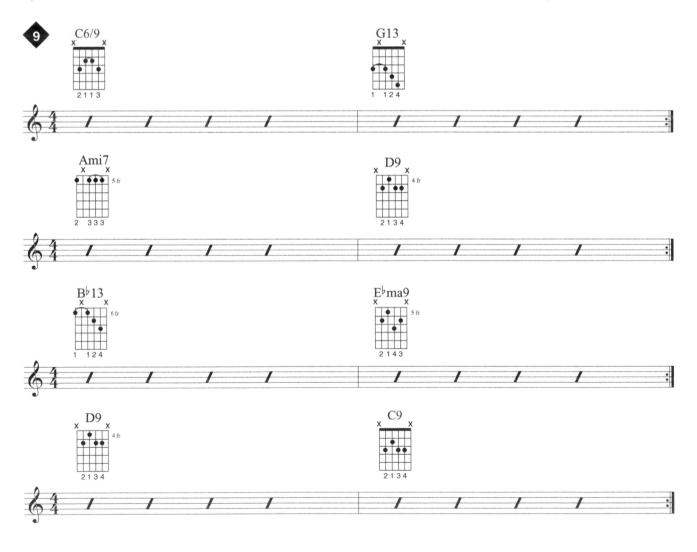

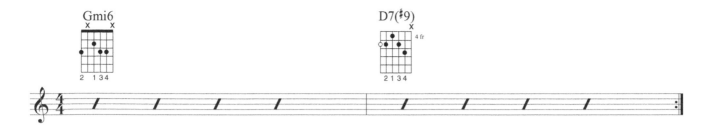

Two-Chords-Per-Measure

Now try anticipation with two-chords-per-measure. This can be difficult and should be practiced a lot before moving on to the next chapter. Notice that you only play the D9 once in each measure—on the upbeat (the "and") of beat 3!

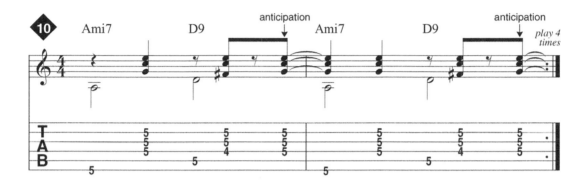

Play the following examples using the one-bar variation with anticipation. Remember: These one-bar patterns must feel totally comfortable so that both your right and left hands are playing with confidence and rhythmic accuracy. Practice slowly, then build up tempo gradually.

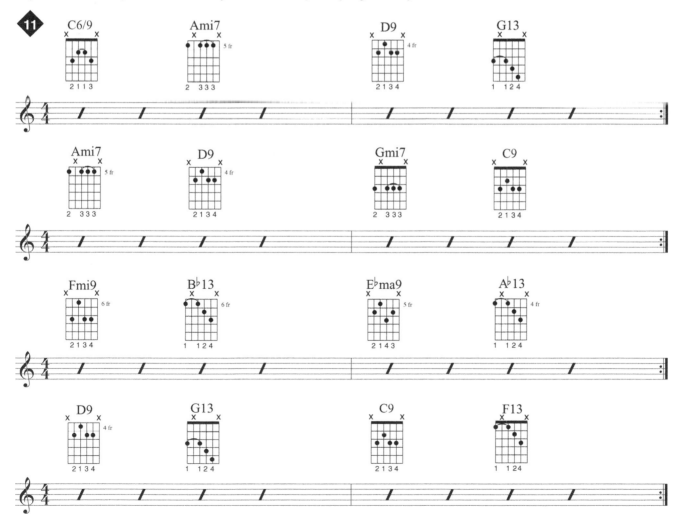

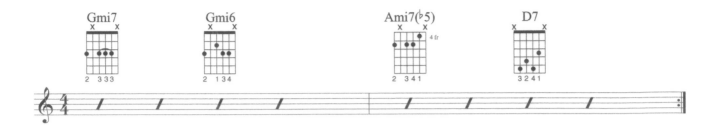

Ultimately, the decision of whether to anticipate or not with these one-bar patterns is yours. The melody and rhythms that you hear are what your ear should base its decisions on. The anticipation gives a little "kick" and syncopation to the overall progression. Familiarity with this comes from repeated listening to Brazilian music and rhythms until you recognize it and it becomes a natural part of the rhythms that you play. This is one of the elements described as "Brazilian swing."

Here's an example of how the three elements we've learned—the one-bar pattern, the one-bar variation, and anticipation—can all be combined into a cohesive guitar part. A typical bossa nova chart might have chords written like example A, but they would be played like example B.

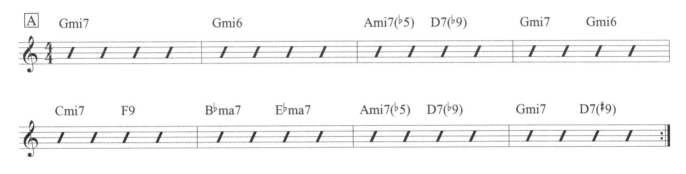

Keep the bass line steady: half notes on the beat. Accent the chord attack to get a syncopated sound.

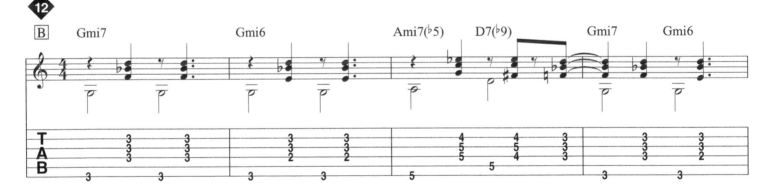

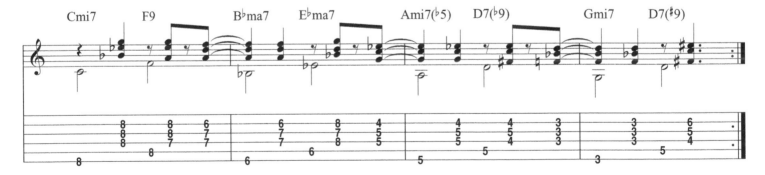

Chapter 2 BOSSA NOVA

TWO-BAR PATTERNS AND BEYOND

Two-bar patterns are another way to add syncopation in the bossa nova style. Since they involve more combinations of downbeat and upbeat than one-bar patterns, more time may be required before you feel comfortable with them. Be patient, and practice slowly!

Here is the basic two-bar rhythm figure. Notice that the second measure is a mirror (reverse) image of the first measure. Cool, huh?

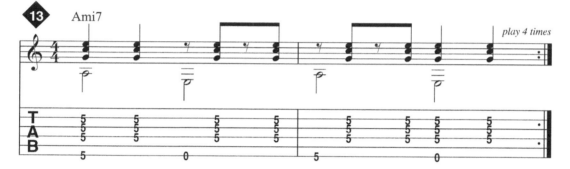

Notice also that now you must use the thumb and fingers together on beat 1 of the first measure and on beat 3 of the second measure. (In the one-bar patterns, the thumb and fingers were always separate.)

Use these next progressions to execute and hear the rhythm pattern accurately. These are each two measures per chord, which gives you plenty of time to focus on your right-hand coordination.

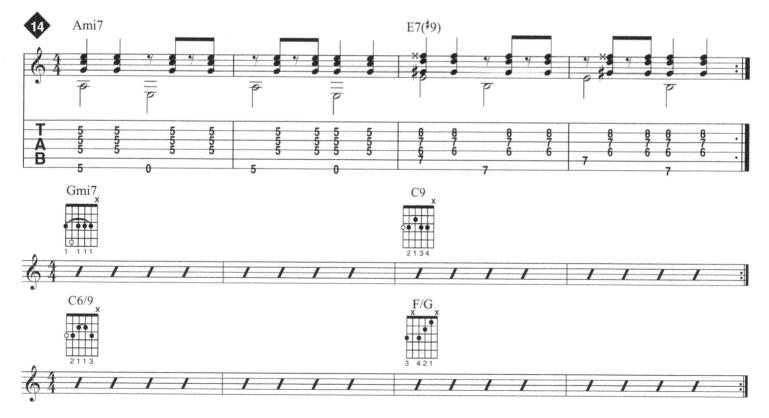

These next one-chord-per-measure progressions require anticipation of the second chord because of the upbeat attack on the "and" of beat 4 in the first measure.

These are two-chords-per-measure. Be careful to anticipate the second measure! Go slowly, and keep the bass in a steady, half-note rhythm.

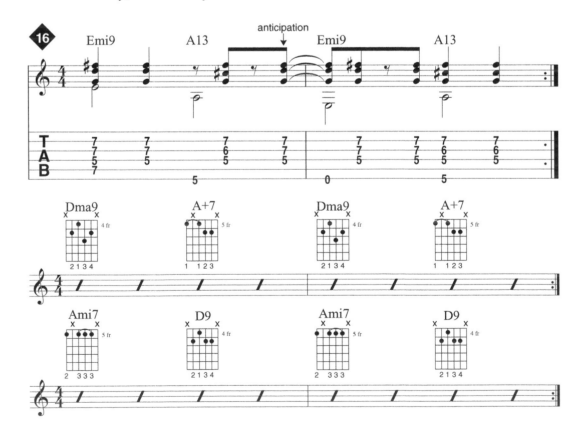

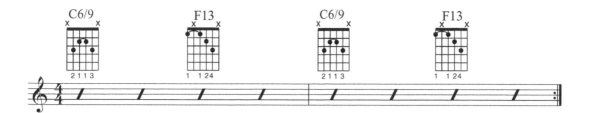

Now try the one-chord-per-measure approach in some typical four-bar progressions. Use the two-bar pattern, but remember that any chord in measures 2 and 4 will be anticipated!

The Reverse Two-Bar Pattern

The next example is the reverse of the original two-bar pattern. Measure 1 is where measure 2 used to be, and vice versa. This may seem like a slight change, but it does alter the overall rhythmic feel.

Now the anticipated chords are in the odd-numbered measures: Measures 1 and 3 are anticipated instead of 2 and 4. You can get lost if you're not aware of the chord changes.

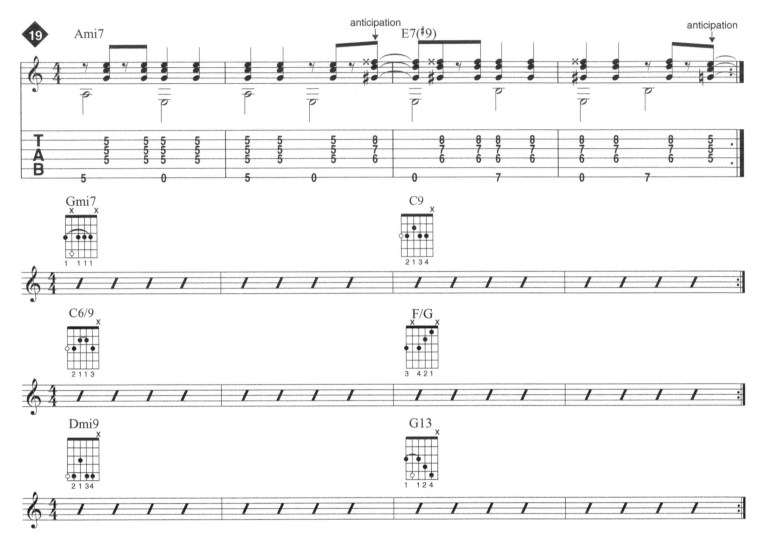

Let's use the same reverse two-bar pattern with one chord per measure. Notice again that the anticipated chord is still in measures 1 and 3.

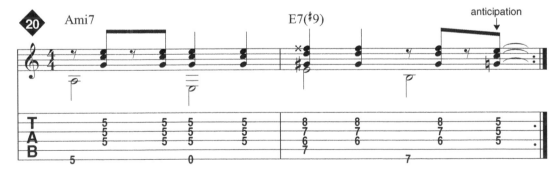

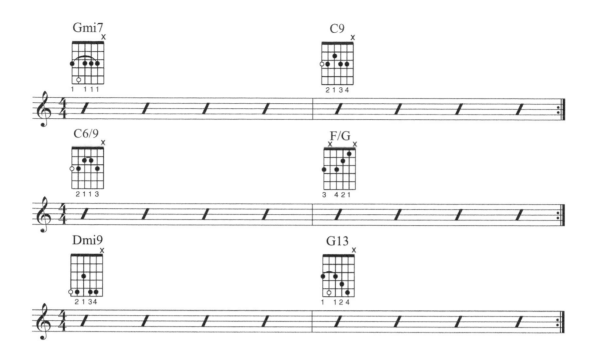

Now try two chords per measure!

Now try this reverse two-bar pattern over different four-bar progressions. The harmonic rhythm is consistent in the first four progressions, but watch out in the last two!

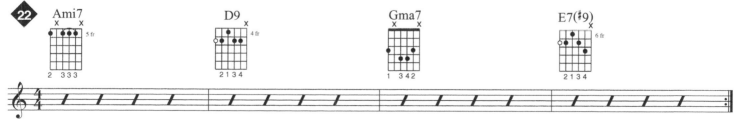

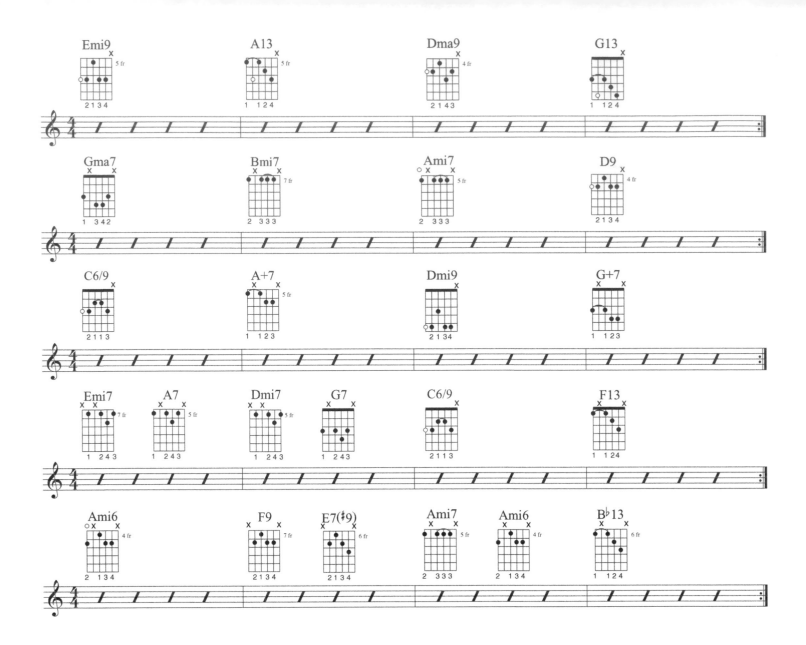

Legato vs. Staccato

You've probably noticed by now that many of these one- and two-bar patterns, while written one way, can actually be played with a variety of nuances. In particular, they can be played *legato,* by not letting up pressure on the chords with your fretting hand (which develops smoothness and evenness), or *staccato,* by quickly releasing the pressure of your fretting hand (which develops the attack and rhythmic accuracy).

This gets to the heart of style, interpretation, and what it means to be a great Latin guitarist. I encourage you to experiment and practice all the rhythms in this book both legato *and* staccato—no matter which way they're written. Your technique and your understanding of Latin rhythms will greatly benefit from it.

Two-Bar Variations

These next two variations are important ones. The first gets us into a "constant eighth-note" feel that is explored in more detail a little bit later, and the second is a variation on the original two-bar pattern that gets us to hear specific accents. These are demanding on the right hand from the standpoint of speed and accuracy, as well as control of your attack dynamics.

Here is the "constant eighth-note pattern" and the "accented pattern":

Use these chord pairs to get the feel of the new patterns. Remember to accent when you use the second pattern!

Extended Patterns

Extended patterns are fill/transition-type figures that work in context with the fundamental patterns; they're generally variations on the fundamental patterns and can be used as a bridge between different grooves. These may feel a little awkward at first, but get the "feel" for each, then try blending them with the fundamental patterns that you've already learned. Don't forget about tempo. Try to vary the tempo to enable your ear to really "hear" the patterns. Also, try them in reverse to hear what that sounds like!

In the second pattern, there is a syncopated bass, which we've not done before. The bass actually follows the rhythmic anticipation: If there is a chord change, the bass anticipates with the chord by playing the root on the upbeat of beat 4 or beat 2.

Thumb and Fingers Together

Thumb and fingers playing together, in unison, is also a part of the bossa nova style. Look at the next group of two-bar patterns as single-line rhythms with no bass part. Your time has to be very good because now you don't have the steady half-note bass rhythm that you had with the other patterns—you must still hear the "2"-feel of the bass, not play it. These patterns are especially effective when playing in a group situation, where a bassist* will be laying down the "2."

To get the unison feel in your right hand, first practice playing quarter notes (both staccato and legato), then shift to eighths, then eventually to sixteenths. Use a metronome, and keep track of your progress using metronome markings. Gradually increase your tempo!

---

* FYI: Playing the earlier patterns with a bass line in them shouldn't get in the way of a bassist if they are played accurately and with good time!

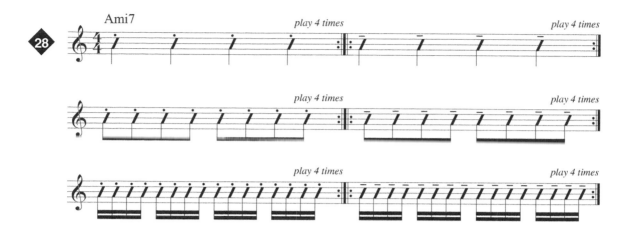

Now try each of these rhythms using the thumb-and-fingers unison technique. Start with just one or two chords in repetition. Eventually, you'll want to apply these rhythms to complete progressions.

Use one of the above patterns for all eight measures of the next example. Eventually, try all seven patterns. When they really feel good, then start to mix and match them with the basic one- and two-bar patterns that you first learned. Sing the pattern as well! You must hear it and feel it against the 4/4 pulse.

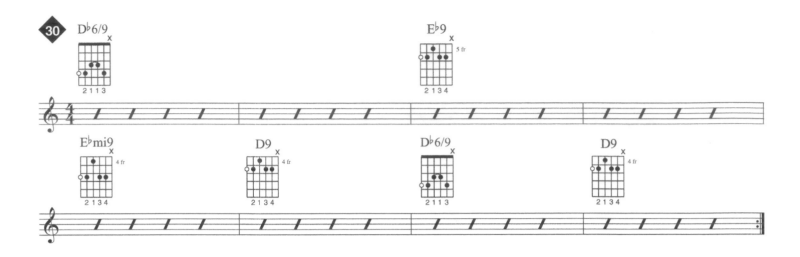

This is a 32-bar tune to workout on. Try all patterns, and then improvise!

31 Bossa Nova 1

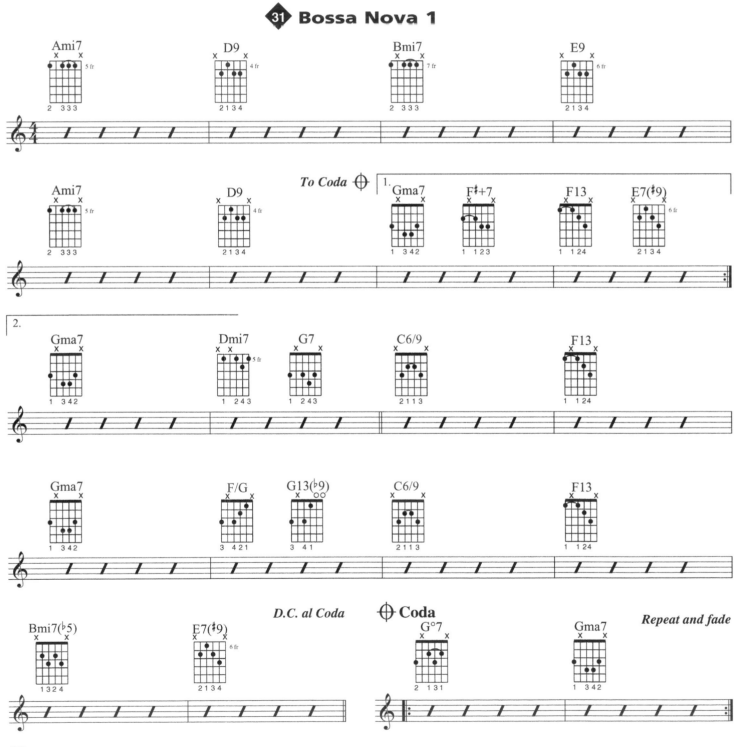

Chapter  SAMBA

Samba is perhaps the best known of all Brazilian grooves. It's also the oldest, which makes it the "mother" of most other Brazilian styles—bossa nova was actually derived from it. We started with bossa nova because the feel is generally a little slower than the samba and therefore easier to learn. Now it's time to try our one- and two-bar bossa nova patterns in the faster "samba" feel. The samba is felt in a "2" beat. It may be written either in 2/2, as is usually the case in America, or in 2/4, which is what is typically used in Brazil. We'll use 2/2 to make it easier to compare with the bossa nova.

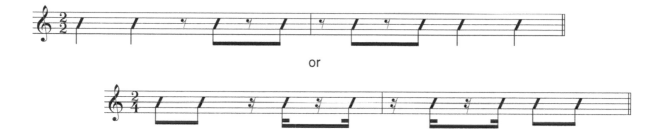

or

The figure below is called the "samba clave." A *clave** is a repeated rhythm pattern that is central to a song; all other rhythms typically relate to it. In particular, this is an example of the *forward samba clave*.

You may be saying to yourself, "But this is the same rhythm that we called the 'two-bar pattern' in the bossa nova—except there's no bass part!" Well, you're correct. The thumb-and-fingers unison style is an integral part of the samba style, and that's why the rhythm is written without the bass notated. But you can also play it with a half-note bass idea as well, as in the bossa nova. Keep in mind, though, that in 2/2 those half notes are occurring on *each beat*—they sound like quarter notes in 4/4. Practice this pattern both ways, and make sure that you are using a metronome:

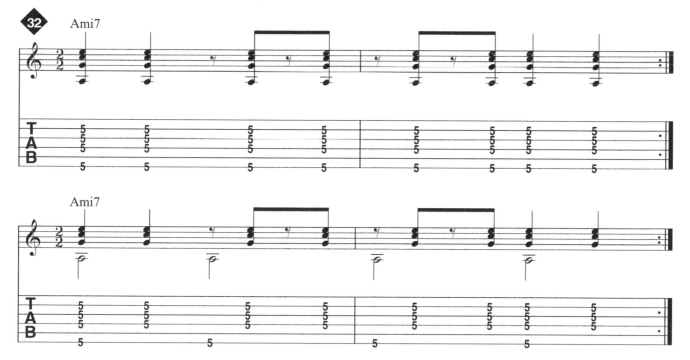

---

* The term *clave* is most often used with Afro-Cuban styles, as it is also the name of an instrument used in that music, while the Brazilian styles don't have that instrument, so the term is not in the language. Here, we are using the term "clave" to mean a repetitive central rhythm pattern.

Here are some two-measures-per-chord progressions to practice the forward samba clave on. Try them both ways, first with thumb-and-fingers unison, then with a chord-and-bass-note approach. Stick with the root only (no 5th) in the bass to keep things moving along smoothly.

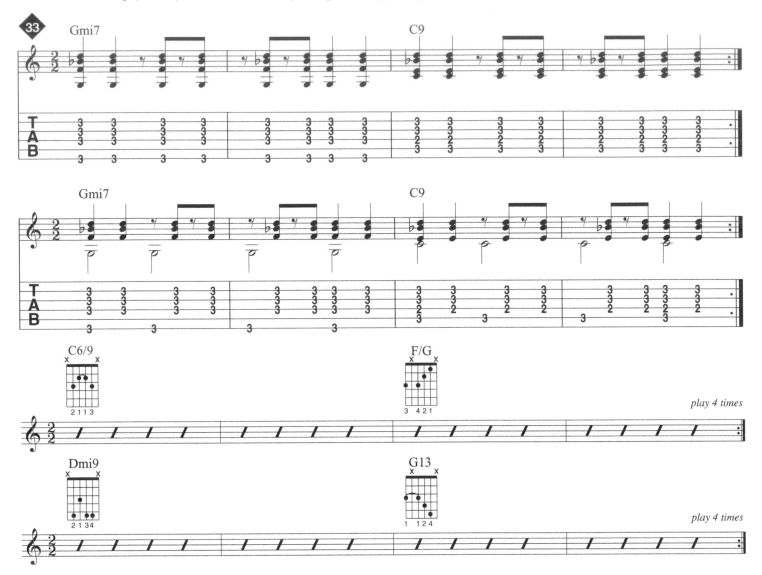

Now try some one-chord-per-measure progressions. (Notice the anticipation of the second chord!)

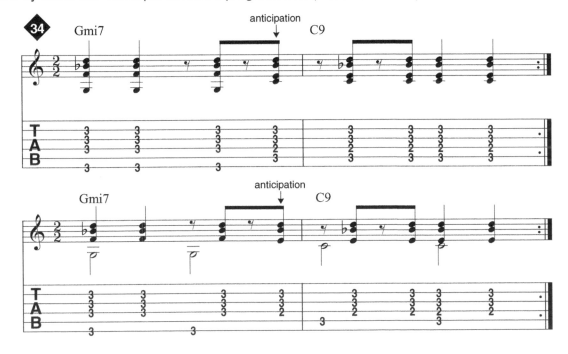

The Reverse Samba Clave

The *reverse samba clave* is just like the reverse two-bar pattern in the bossa nova: Measure 1 of the forward pattern becomes becomes measure 2 of the reverse pattern, and vice versa. It changes the feel quite a bit.

Try the reverse samba clave on some two-chord-per-measure progressions. (Watch the anticipations!)

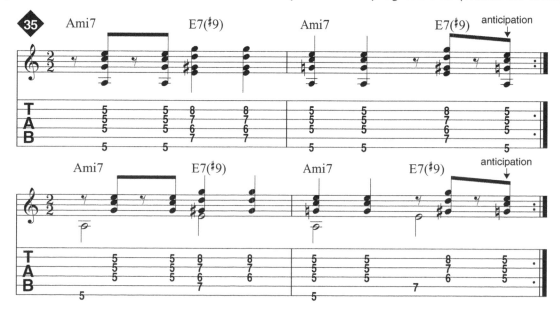

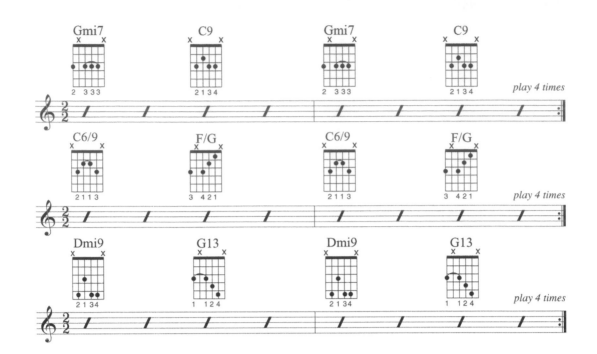

You can practice any of the previous bossa nova progressions with a 2/2 samba feel. When you do that, you start to get a good sense for the difference between the bossa nova and samba rhythms.

🔷36 Samba Too

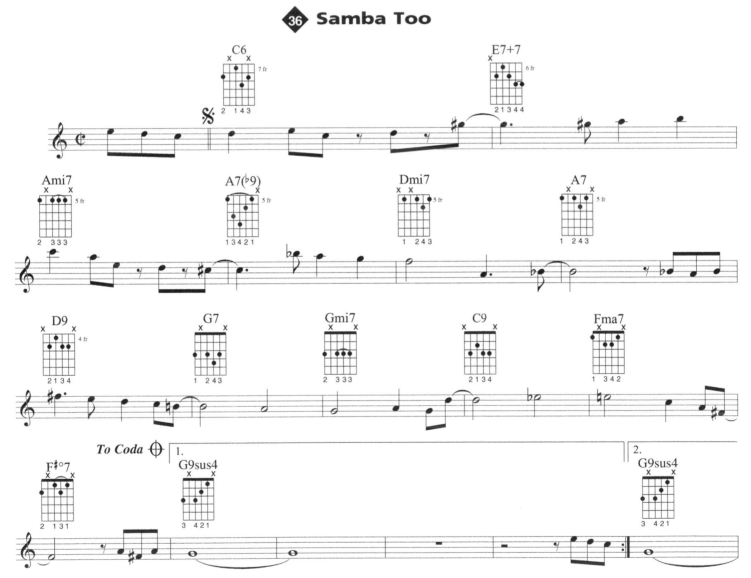

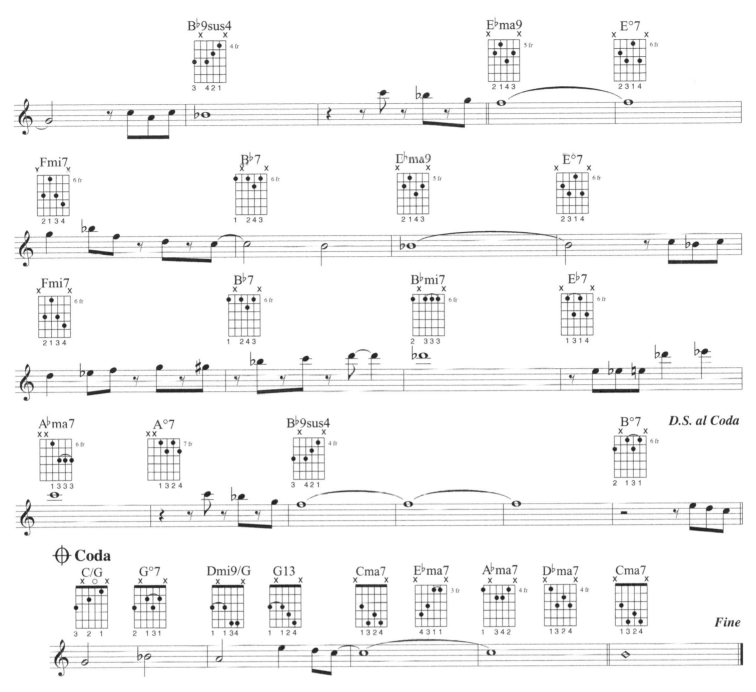

The Constant Eighth-Note Style

The style of playing where the thumb and fingers attack the strings together is very much part of the samba feel, and it lends itself to a driving kind of rhythm that is unique to the Brazilian sound: *the constant eighth-note style.*

This is a very percussive feel that uses a lot of the same rhythms we have already discussed, as well as rhythms typical of the percussion instruments. It's not easy because of the tempos and use of accents. Repetitive patterns are used, but the sound also has a free use of rhythm where attacks and accents are mixed up in an improvisational way. You must be familiar with the style to be able to improvise and mix patterns together to create a nice flow. This is similar to the way jazz uses a free style of comping (accompaniment) when backing a vocal or soloist. It's also similar to funk in that you are constantly plucking strings with the right hand, but accenting only selected chord strikes.

There are actually two ways to achieve the "constant eighth-note" sound:

1.) Accent some attacks to make them louder, so that they stick out from the softer attacks—a function of the right hand.

2.) Completely mute the softer attacks, and play the accented attacks with a normal touch—a function of the left hand.

Try this with some chords; first, use the right-hand "accent" method, then try the left-hand "attack and mute" method. Make sure your time is steady and that you're feeling the half-note pulse.

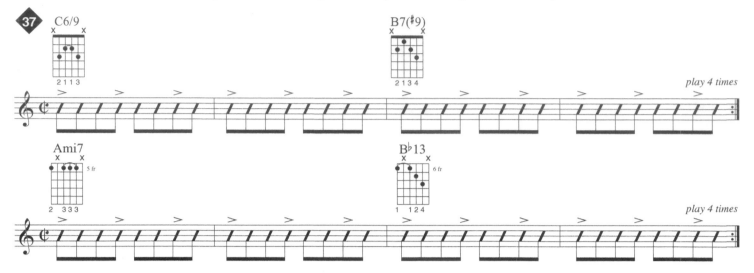

Pick Your Pattern

Notice the underlying pattern in the previous examples? It's a new one for us, but a common percussion figure in Brazilian music:

Any pattern can be played using the constant eighth-note style. Play the following two-bar patterns in the constant eighth-note style, even though only the attacks are written out. You decide which sound that you want:

- accented (loud/soft)
- muted (attack/mute)

38 Bossa nova clave pattern

Reverse bossa vova clave pattern

Samba clave pattern

Reverse samba clave pattern

Variation

Though the "constant eighth-note" style is mostly associated with the samba feel, it is also used in the slower bossa nova (4/4) feel as well as some slower samba grooves such as *samba canseo*, which means "lazy samba," a slower "2" feel.

Try any of the previous patterns on the following progressions. Remember that the ideas discussed about chord anticipation still apply to this "constant eighth-note" style, as well as when using a bass note style of accompaniment. Strive to get the accented attack feel first, then try the muted approach!

More Patterns

Here are the two-bar "thumb-and-fingers" patterns discussed previously in relation to the bossa nova feel. Now the difference is to play them in the samba "2" feel with the new constant eighth-note style. Use both approaches: accented (loud/soft) and muted (attack/mute).

These patterns and styles take some time to master, so stay with each pattern and pick up a new one every week or so. Play lots of progressions with every pattern that you learn. There are many here, and they should each be practiced many times to get comfortable with them. (When you have the above patterns under your fingers, try them on the progressions on Track 39.)

Eventually, you can mix your approaches. You can even mix this style with the bass-note-and-chord approach—maybe you want a different chordal texture for a different part of a song, say the "B" section or the bridge/chorus. This offers a contrast in your accompaniment. Ultimately, you can improvise all these patterns in various combinations and textures; however, it is important to make sure you can play all the individual rhythm patterns with ease and authority before trying to improvise combinations of them.

Chapter 4 VARIATIONS

PARTIDO ALTO, BAIÃO, AND 3/4 BOSSA NOVA

Partido alto is a type of funky samba that is played in more urban areas with smaller ensembles. There is a syncopated bass part that typically accompanies the guitar, but here is the samba variation for the guitar by itself:

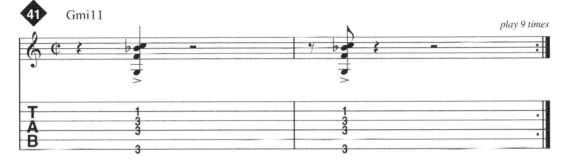

This next pattern has the even half note in the bass for guitar. You may remember this one from the thumb-and-fingers patterns—now with the addition of a root/5th bass.

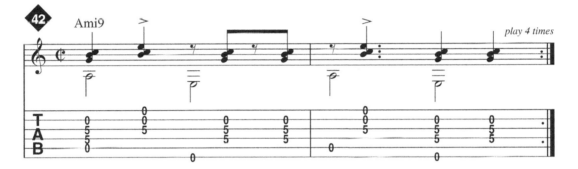

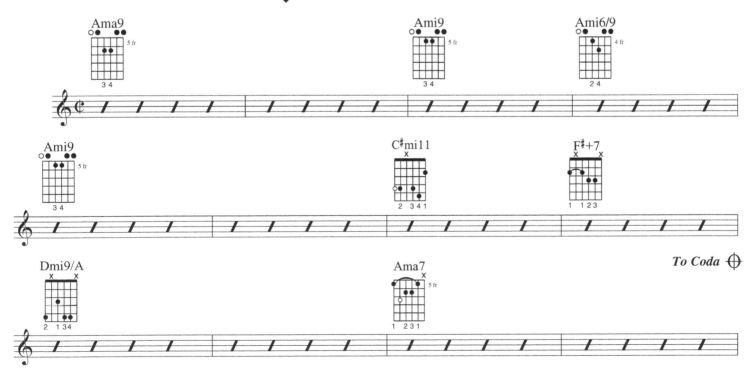

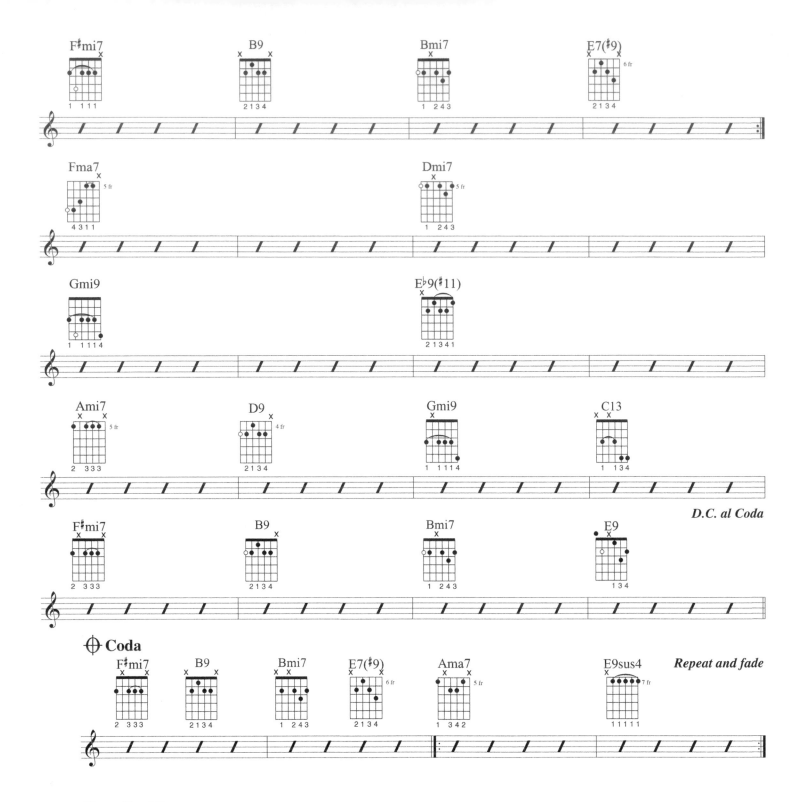

The Baião

The *baião* is a rhythm from northern Brazil. It has a common figure in it that is also in many other styles, but here it is played with the Brazilian "feel" and interpretation.

The guitar part in a baião typically consists of just two attacks, while the bass plays a distinctive root/5th pattern, doubled by the kick drum:

You can combine the two parts to make a solo guitar part that has chords with this bass line figure:

3/4 Bossa Nova

Another variation is the 3/4 bossa nova. This is rare, but it sounds great and gives us a new outlook on 3/4 time, which is normally so connected to the waltz feel. Here, it is distinctly Brazilian!

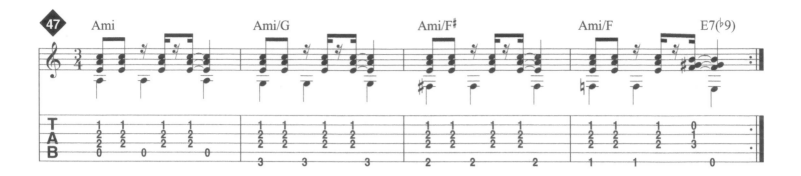

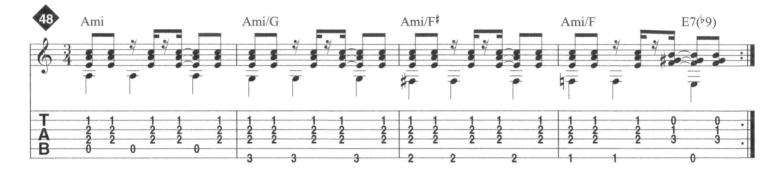

Using different string sets in the right hand gives a nice sound. Even though these examples are written with sixteenth rests, let the strings ring out over each other. (It's just easier to read this way!)

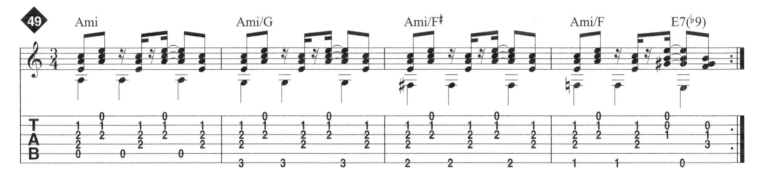

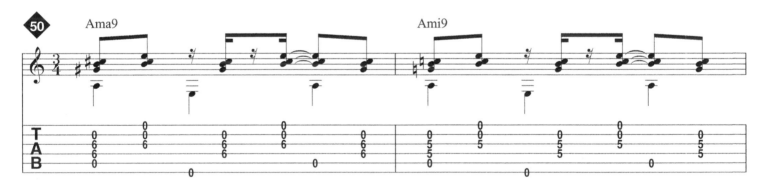

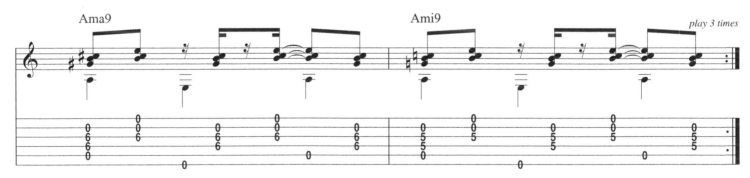

Part Two
Afro-Cuban Rhythms

Rhythms that come from Cuba, Puerto Rico, the Dominican Republic, Jamaica, and other Caribbean nations make up what is generally referred to as "Afro-Cuban" Latin music. These have a different feel and style of their own that is distinct from the Brazilian sound. Only repeated listening will allow you to instantly recognize the difference between Afro-Cuban or Brazilian "Latin" styles.

Other terms used to describe this music include Afro-Caribbean, or sometimes just the word "salsa." There are many small subdivisions of the style; however, the concept presented here is to learn the most common rhythms and learn them well—only then can you move on to advanced material. As we take a look at these essential rhythms, you'll notice they move from slower to faster. These rhythms are based on tempo, and as the tempo rises, the patterns change to establish a nice groove at that tempo range:

slower		faster
Bolero	Cha cha	Mambo
$\frac{4}{4}$	Nanigo 6/8	$\frac{2}{2}$

Chapter 5 BOLERO

Bolero is the Latin ballad. Generally speaking, boleros are slow, romantic tunes that should be played with a relaxed feel. The distinctive drum pattern may be mimicked on the guitar, or you may accompany with half notes or whole notes only. You may even play with a "jazz" ballad feel. This is a situation in which you want to keep your ears open and play what is appropriate.

Here is the drum/guitar pattern:

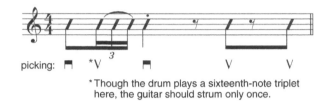

*Though the drum plays a sixteenth-note triplet here, the guitar should strum only once.

Use the next two I–IV and I–II–V chord progressions to get the bolero rhythm solid. You might not always play every attack all the time, but to practice the rhythm, try to play it consistently and evenly throughout the song. Good chordal backing should use some half notes and whole notes as well.

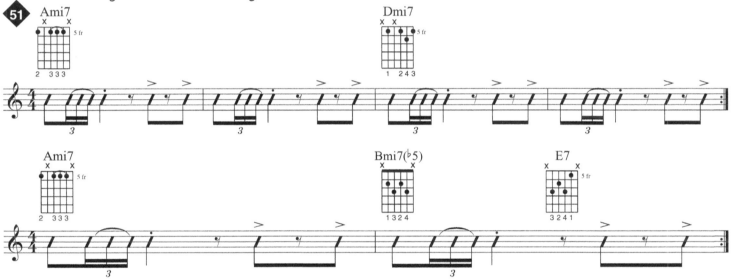

Now try a little progression that starts out with the I-to-IV in A minor, but then modulates to the relative key of C major.

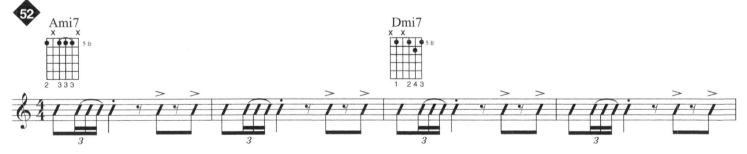

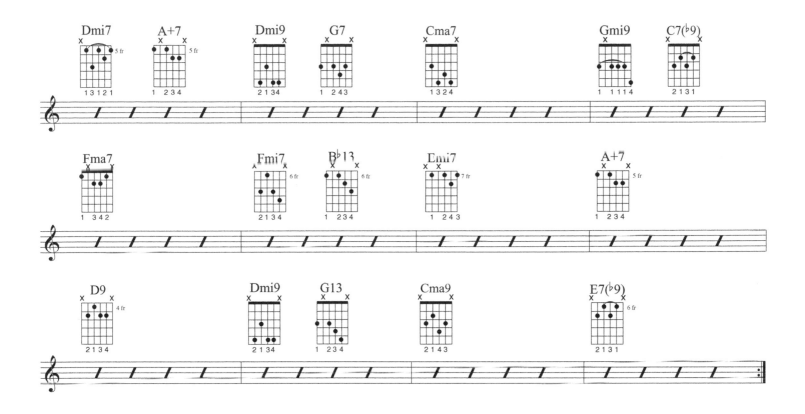

Chapter 6 CHA CHA

oving up in tempo a little, we come to the next groove, called cha cha. This is from the Cuban dance of the same name. The feel is 4/4, and a constant quarter note is usually played on the cowbell.

Try maintaining this pattern over some progressions—first, two-measures-per chord. This is a thumb-and-fingers unison, or "block chord," approach to playing the cha cha.

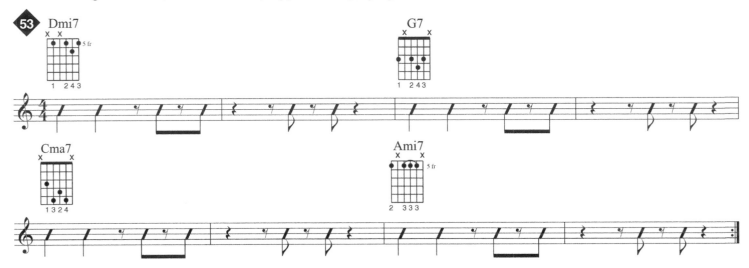

Now try one chord per measure and use the rhythm anticipation on the upbeat of 4. This anticipation is necessary when a new chord arrives in the second measure.

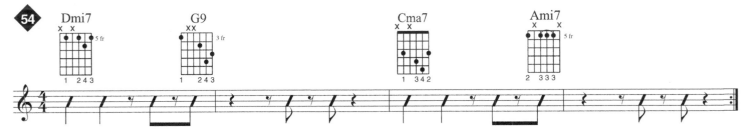

Now try a progression that has some extensions and alterations.

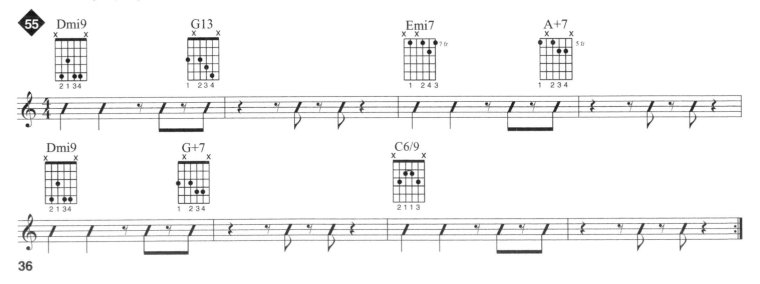

Chordal Interpretations

The next step is to interpret the chords in a combination of single notes and double stops and/or three-note voicings. You'll notice that the rhythm for most of these patterns is the same; however, variations can and do occur. Work on the rhythm until you can play it easily and can clap it while listening to a cha-cha tune.

The trick here is to understand how the notes interpret the chord symbol. First just learn the patterns, then figure out how the tones relate to the chord.

This first idea works as a vamp that moves from the ♭7th-to-6th over a minor chord.

Here's one that moves 7th-to-6th for a major sound.

Here are two more approaches to playing on a minor vamped chord: the familiar "root-to-major 7th-to minor 7th-and back," and a variation, which goes down to the 6th.

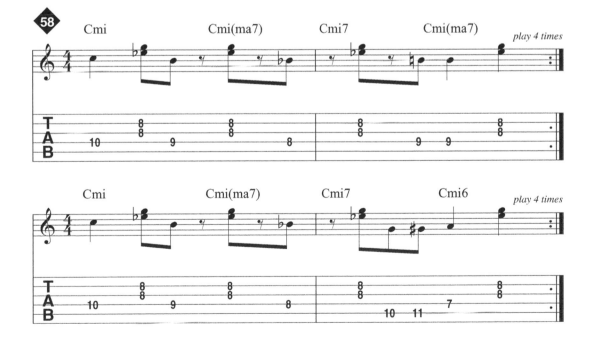

Short ii-V Progressions

While some of these patterns work well on a static C minor chord, they can also relate to an F chord, making them suitable for a common ii-V progression. As a ii-V sound, they are seen as short ii-V because they are two beats each:

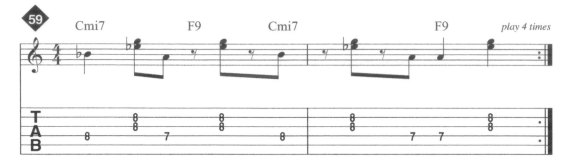

Add a B♭ vamp at the end, and you have a ii-V-I progression in B♭!

Long ii-V Progressions

Now let's look at long ii-V's. These are four beats each. They're all variations of each other: The chord forms remain the same while the single lines that approach them vary.

Now it's ii-V-I-IV7.

Variations

Make sure to practice the examples shown in C minor in other keys as well. Also, learn all examples on string sets 4-2 and 3-1. Get to a point where you can switch between short ii-V and the long ii-V. Play various combinations (long/short, different string sets) of the ii-V chord progressions.

Here's an example of long/short ii-V's mixed with root movement:

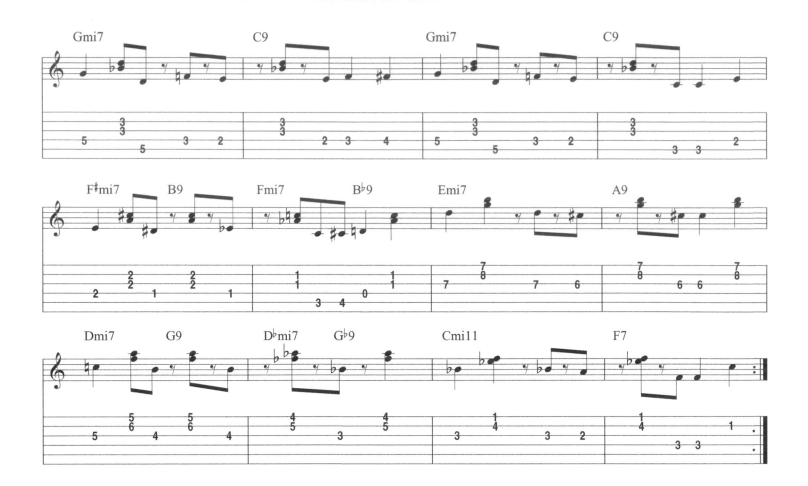

The next step would be to add the I chord with the ii-V's. If the ii-V progression leads to the intended I chord, then it's called a *resolving ii-V*. If it does not lead to the intended tonic, then it is called a *nonresolving ii-V*.

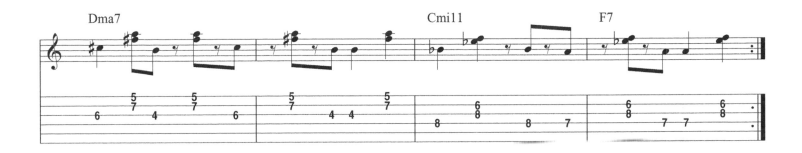

Here are some variations in the key of G major. Try these in other keys as well! Keep practicing until it's automatic. Use a drum machine, and seek out percussionist friends to practice with. This takes time to begin to interpret in this manner. Work hard on each individual pattern and keep track of your tempos (♩ = 60-100).

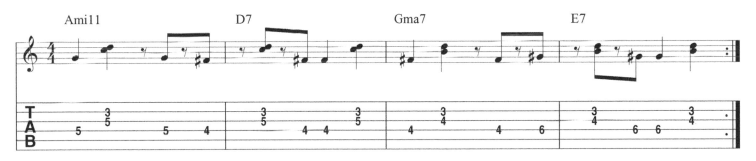

Bass Line with Root

So far, we have left the root out of the bass, instead using movements of 7ths and 6ths, or 3rds. These voicings are the correct ones for playing with a bassist, where the root motion is already taken care of by someone else. Sometimes, however, we may want the root motion to be in our guitar part. Here is an example with that in mind. This concept is great for solo guitar.

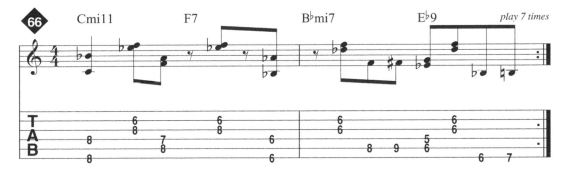

Chapter 7 MAMBO

Moving faster still, we arrive at the tempo where 4/4 becomes 2/2. The half note is the pulse, and many of the patterns that were used in the cha cha (4/4) now work in the mambo feel (2/2). Practice all the following patterns slowly in 4/4 before you work them up to the "2" feel of the mambo. Once you feel comfortable in 2/2, begin to speed up the tempo. Tap your foot! Remember: these are dance rhythms, and you must keep a steady pulse and play relaxed.

Try this in 2/2, and learn to read progressions with this rhythm only.

Remember to anticipate the chord in the second measure of the two-measure phrase.

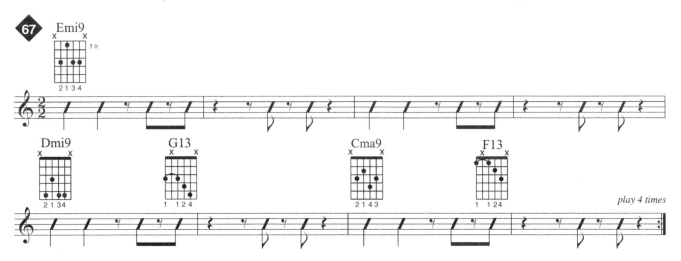

Chordal Interpretations

Here is a chordal interpretation for I–ii, a common progression to vamp on. Start in 4/4, but soon get the tempo up to a cut-time or 2/2 feel. This is more in line with the tempo of the mambo. Remember to see it on string set 4-1 as well as string set 5-2.

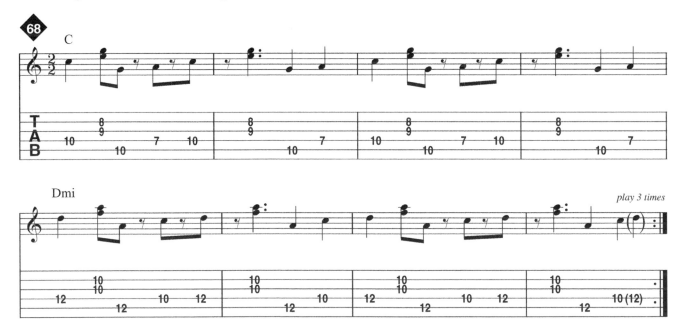

42

This is a variation on the previous I–ii pattern.. Remember to do all examples in different keys.

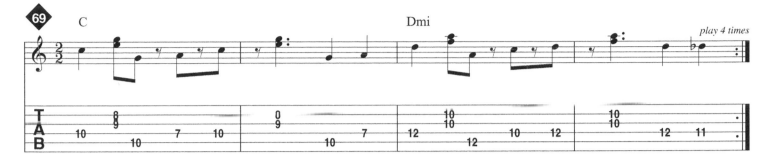

Here's i-iv. It's the same move down a 5th interval. You could also go up a 4th to get the iv (Gmi) chord. This relates to the string-set idea:

- String set 3-1 for the i chord, go down a 5th for iv chord on string set 4-2
- String set 4-2 for the i chord, go up a 4th for iv chord on string set 3-1.

This works for major and minor.

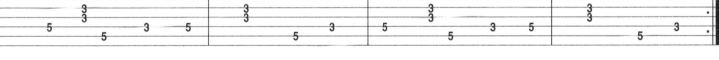

Now, try this idea on I-ii in D major. Notice the chromatic walkdown.

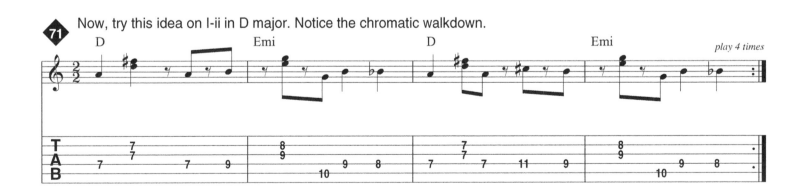

Here's iv-i in B minor.

I-IV-V is the backbone of the Afro-Cuban style. Try these variations and move them to different keys.

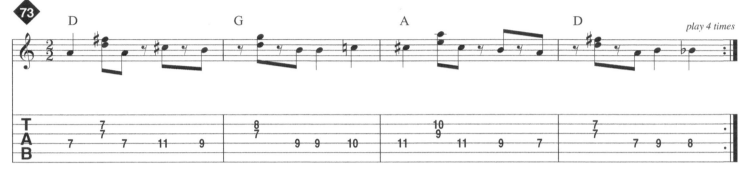

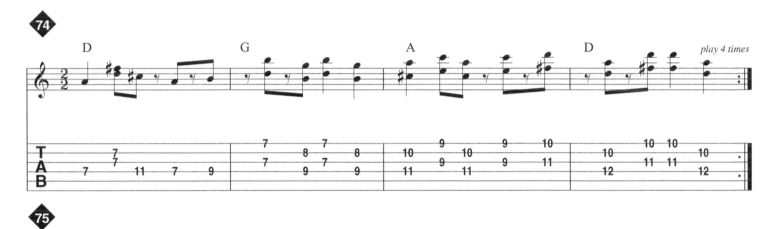

Vamps

76 Mambo #1

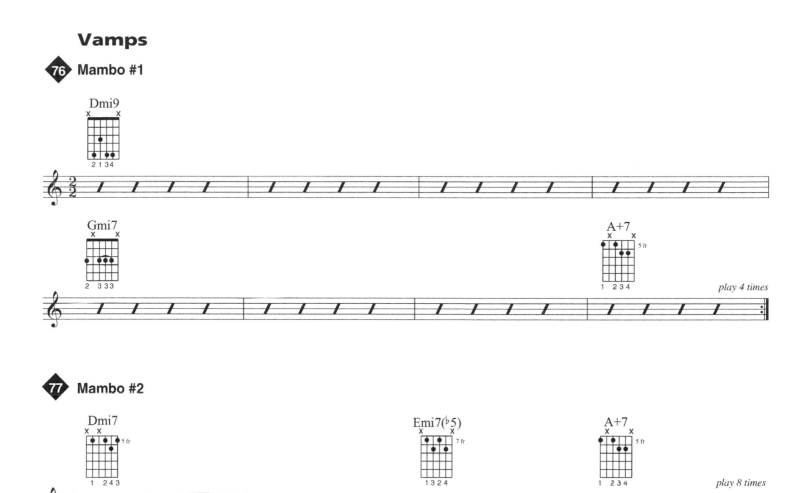

77 Mambo #2

Chapter  NANIGO 6/8

he nanigo rhythm is not bound by the tempo; it can range from slow to fast. Sometimes referred to as the "Afro" feel because of its polyrhythmic sound, the 6/8 time signature has a pulse of two beats per bar, which are each subdivided into three (triplets). The rhythms below are called "bell" patterns. They define the nanigo rhythm.

Clap these while tapping your foot in "2."

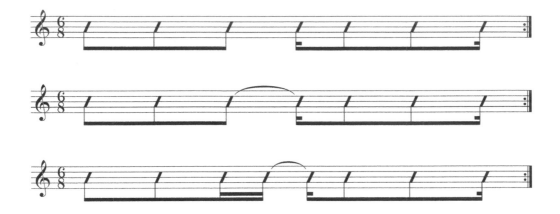

6/8 Minor Blues

Here's a 6/8 minor blues that is typical of the nanigo feel. Does this sound familiar? Below is a sample bass line and guitar part.

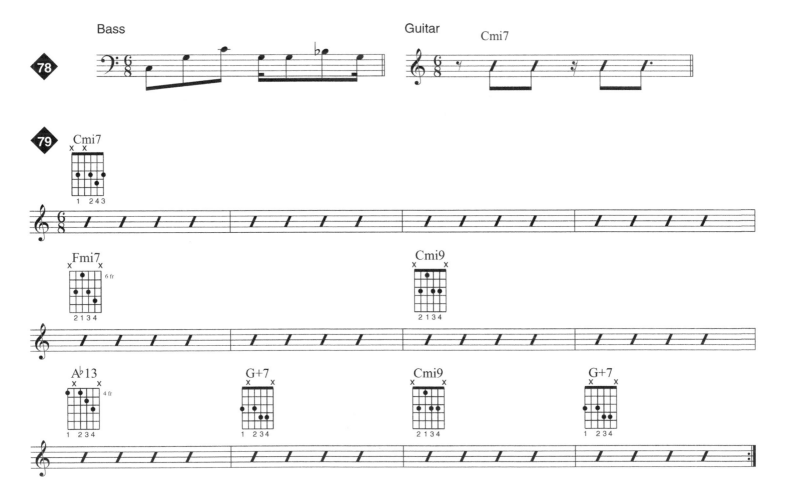

DRUMSET PATTERNS

The following drumset patterns were used on the audio tracks. They are included here to help you better understand how each rhythm works—as well as to give your drummer ideas for what to play if you are practicing Latin rhythms in a band situation.

Brazilian

Afro-Cuban

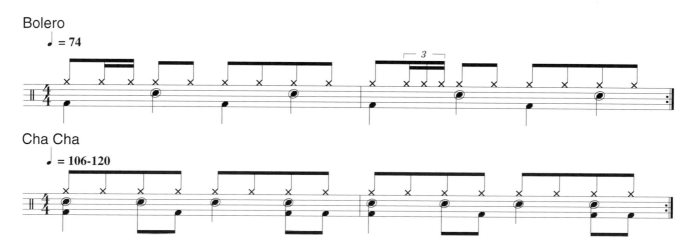

Mambo

Mambo 1 and 2 (vamps)

Nanigo

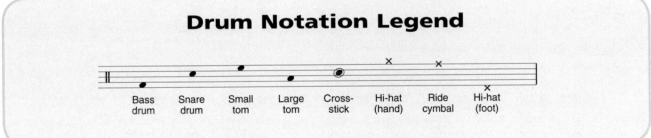

Drum Notation Legend

Bass drum   Snare drum   Small tom   Large tom   Cross-stick   Hi-hat (hand)   Ride cymbal   Hi-hat (foot)